This bite-sized bo[illegible]
useful overview of [illegible]
achieve the follow[illegible]

- Define the me[illegible]
- Understand th[illegible]
- Appreciate the [illegible] relationships
- Learn ways to practise and demonstrate empathy
- Be more inclusive and make a positive impact

Empathy is seeing with the eyes of another, listening with the ears of another, and feeling with the heart of another
Anonymous

What is empathy?

Empathy is our ability to sense other people's emotions and understand how they may be feeling. It is about seeing things from another person's perspective and imagining ourselves in their position.

Practising empathy helps us to connect and relate well with other people in our lives. The term empathy was first introduced in 1909 by psychologist Edward B Titchener as a translation of the German term einfühlung which means "feeling into".

Empathy is a skill like any other human skill. If you get a chance to practice, you can get better at it

Simon Baron Cohen

Why is empathy important?

Humans are social beings, and we all have the capacity to develop empathy which enables us to build stronger and more supportive relationships. Like any behavioural skill, empathy can be cultivated through intentional effort and practice.

By being empathetic we can better “read” another person’s inner state and interpret it without blaming, giving advice or attempting to fix the situation. It also helps us to embrace diversity and to be more inclusive.

Wherever there is a
human being there is an
opportunity for kindness
Seneca

Kindness and empathy

Being empathetic is a form of kindness and helps us to consider and care about the wellbeing of others. To truly empathise and understand another individual is an intuitive act where we give complete attention to someone else's experience by pushing aside our own issues.

By being empathetic and understanding we can support others in feeling psychologically safe enough to share openly and honestly. This will also help the other person to feel that they are not entirely isolated and enable them to recover and grow stronger in the knowledge that they have a kind and caring supporter.

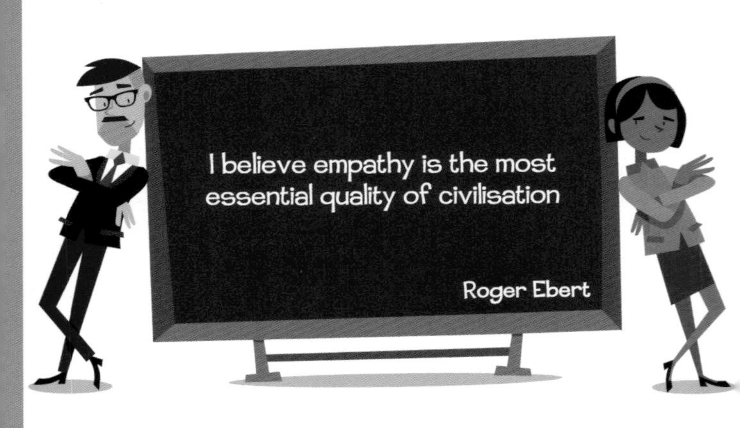
I believe empathy is the most essential quality of civilisation
Roger Ebert

Types of empathy

There are different types of empathy that a person may experience:

Affective empathy - This involves our ability to understand another person's emotions and respond appropriately.

Somatic empathy - This involves having a physical reaction in response to what someone else experiences.

Cognitive empathy - This involves being able to understand another person's mental state and what they may be thinking in response to their situation.

Empathy is really important and only when our clever brain and our human heart work together in harmony can we achieve our true potential

Jane Goodall

Empathy and the brain

Various studies have shown that specific areas of our brain can play a role in how we experience empathy. In recent years social neuroscientists have made considerable progress in revealing the mechanisms that enable us to feel what another person is feeling.

MRI (magnetic resonance imaging) scans have shown that when a highly empathetic person observes another person experiencing a variety of emotions, the empath's brain fires off the same neural circuits. This can make them actually feel what the other person is feeling.

Empathy and wellbeing

By being empathetic we can boost our helping behaviours through a deep desire to support other people. It is important however to bear in mind that without healthy boundaries empathetic people can sometimes become overwhelmed and even overstimulated from always thinking about other people's emotions.

Asking yourself the following five questions can be helpful in understanding your own needs so that you can be aware of your own wellbeing:

1. How much space and solitude do I need to feel well?
2. What refreshes and recharges me?
3. What drains me?
4. When do I feel my worst?
5. When do I feel my best?

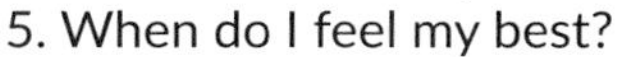

Empathy and meditation

Meditation may also increase our empathy by raising self-awareness. Researchers from Emory University have discovered that compassion meditation can improve our ability to empathise. Meditation for empathy does this by activating areas of our brain associated with compassion.

Empathy is an understanding of the shared human condition and this is intrinsically attached to the unfolding nature of our own kindness and compassion. Meditation calms the nervous system and helps us to become more aware of our own emotions, which in turn helps us to be able to empathise better with others.

How empathetic are you?

Do you care deeply about other people?
Are you good at listening to what others have to say?
Can you sense how other people are feeling?
Do you often think about how other people feel?
Do other people come to you for advice or for help with their problems?
Do you try to help others who are suffering?
Can you tell when people aren't being honest?
Are you able to set healthy boundaries in your relationships with other people?

The next few pages offer some useful tips and suggestions on ways to practise empathy.

How to be empathetic

True empathy requires that you step outside your own emotions to view things entirely from the perspective of the other person
Anonymous

Expand your world view

Our world view is a framework of beliefs, values and attitudes which affects everything we perceive, think, feel and do. As we evolve we can become restricted by the boundaries of what we experience, so constantly expanding our world view will help us to be more empathetic.

Reading things that we don't necessarily agree with or instigating conversations with people that challenge our perspective is a good place to start. Expanding our horizons by embracing new experiences will also help us to develop as well-rounded, balanced and inclusive human beings. By keeping an open mind and open heart we will be able to constantly learn and grow.

Learning to stand in somebody else's shoes, to see through their eyes, that's how peace begins. And it's up to you to make that happen. Empathy is a quality of character that can change the world

Barack Obama

Put yourself in others' shoes

To practise empathy there is a very useful skill that can help called "perspective taking". This is about consciously putting ourselves in someone else's shoes and imagining what challenges they might be facing and how it could be making them feel, think and behave.

This mindset shift helps to ensure that we stay in an empathic state. By attempting to imagine what it would be like to experience what they are going through helps us to gain a better understanding of things from their point of view. These shared emotional experiences help us to relate to and gain a clearer perspective of the other person's situation.

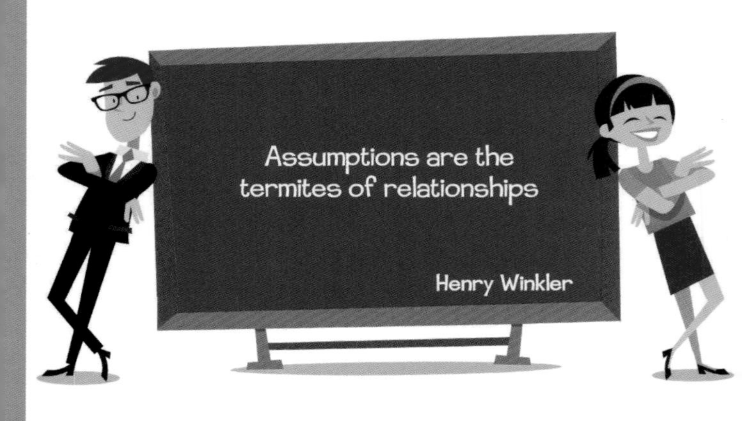
Assumptions are the termites of relationships
Henry Winkler

Challenge assumptions

We all hold unconscious beliefs and bias, and this could well be about various social and identity groups. This bias is triggered by the brain making quick judgments and assessments of people and situations. Often this is influenced by our own background, societal stereotypes and personal experience.

To be truly empathetic we need to constantly be aware of and challenge our biases about people and stereotyping. We may well discover that many of the assumptions we make are based on erroneous information. Educating ourselves and listening to the groups that are affected by this misinformation is a really good place to start. This is especially important in a world that will thrive through empathy and embracing diversity and inclusivity.

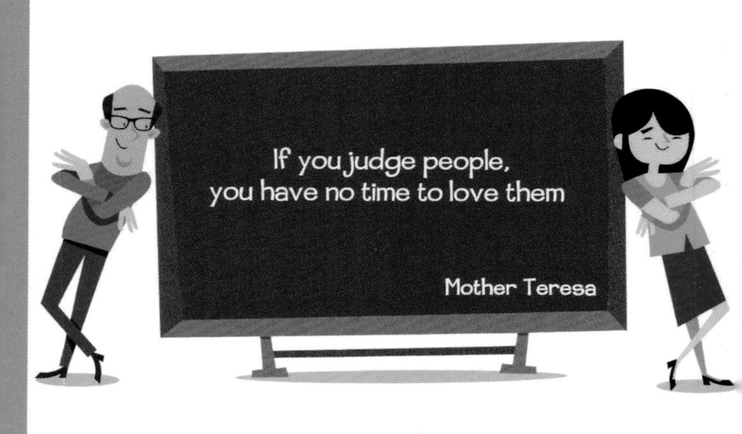
If you judge people,
you have no time to love them
Mother Teresa

Be curious

A valuable trait of empathy is being interested in other people, especially people that we may know nothing about and who are outside of our immediate social and cultural circle. Being curious enables us to seek out challenges and new experiences so that we can broaden our horizons. Curiosity is the gateway to wisdom and life is never dull for a curious person with a growth mindset.

Being curious rather than judgmental about people is a great place to start and finding everyone we meet interesting can be the catalyst for some great conversations. Remember, everyone we meet in our life knows something we don't, so let the adventure begin.

One of the most valuable things
we can do to heal one another
is listen to each other's stories
Rebecca Falls

Be fully present

Being fully present requires us to make a conscious decision to give the other person our undivided attention. So being aware of any potential distractions is important, as well as setting aside our own internal mind chatter so that we can focus on what the other person is saying.

Empathetic people have a way of making us feel as if we are the only person in the room. This is also a sign of respect and can be quite a rarity in today's hyper-distracted world.

Friends are those rare people
who ask how we are,
and then wait to hear the answer
Ed Cunningham

Listen actively

Listening is one of the most powerful and constructive ways that we can demonstrate empathy. When we practise active listening, we are listening with purpose and with a deep desire to want to really hear what someone is saying. Empathetic people take the time to understand the other person's priorities and motivations.

To do this it is important to stay focused and use active listening skills to gain insight. Examples of active listening can be paraphrasing to demonstrate understanding as well as using non-verbal cues such as nodding, eye contact and leaning forward. Brief verbal affirmations can also help to encourage people to be more open and share what is on their mind and how they feel.

The word 'listen' contains the same letters as the word 'silent'
Alfred Brendel

Respect silence

How comfortable are you with a pause in a conversation and a moment of silence? In an attempt to be helpful sometimes we may feel the urge to fill the void and jump in to finish people's sentences, offer them some advice, or even interrupt. Silence can be a very powerful way to simply "be" with another person and allow them the space to collect their thoughts and feel calm. This may be especially helpful when the other person is emotional and troubled.

Being comfortable with pauses in conversation and allowing a moment of silence can also communicate acceptance of how the other person may be in that given moment.

Acknowledge emotions

When we acknowledge something it means we are recognising its value and importance. Emotional validation involves understanding and showing acceptance of how another person may be feeling. This helps the person we are empathising with to know that their feelings are being seen, heard and accepted.

Emotional acknowledgment can help us to establish rapport and interpersonal trust. It can also help others to define how they may be feeling and encourage them. By allowing emotions to flow freely it can also help people to release pent up stress and ultimately feel calmer.

Tune into non-verbal communication

Non-verbal communication provides clues to unspoken and underlying concerns and emotions. It can reinforce or contradict what is being said and it is important to remember that communication runs far deeper than words alone.

During a conversation we may observe the other person dodging eye contact, tensing up or shifting about awkwardly. These are important non-verbal signs, and we will then be able to use our powers of empathy by gently asking the other person to describe what is happening for them. This will encourage them to share their feelings openly, knowing that they won't be judged or criticised.

An empathic person is a good listener, patient, understanding, and kind
Laura Raskin

Question empathetically

Empathetic questioning is asking questions with the intention of seeking to understand how someone is feeling. This helps the other person to express what is really going on and can also help them to understand their own situation better.

We need to ensure that we probe gently rather than bombarding people, so it doesn't sound like an interrogation. So, we need to be mindful of our tone of voice, body language, the way we frame the questions and how we listen and respond.

Here are some examples of empathetic questions:

- How do you feel about this?
- How is this situation affecting you?
- What does this mean to you?
- Why do you think it is making you feel like this?

Use empathetic language

The language we use and the tone we adopt is a major step toward cultivating an empathic attitude. Being tactful and diplomatic is very important and this is the subtle and skilful art of handling a delicate interaction with sensitivity and emotional intelligence. It helps us to be able to tell the truth in a way that considers other people's feelings and reactions. It also helps us to communicate sensitive information by saying things in a way that will preserve and strengthen relationships.

Here are some examples of empathetic language:

- I am so sorry that you are experiencing this
- This does sound really challenging for you
- I can only imagine what you must be going through
- Please know that you have my support and I am here to listen

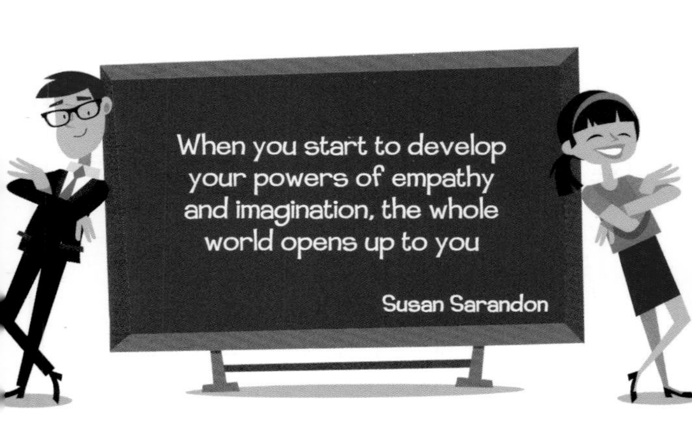
When you start to develop your powers of empathy and imagination, the whole world opens up to you
Susan Sarandon

EMPATHY

How to understand how other people fe

Empathy begins with a deep desire to want to understand life fron someone else's perspective

Liggy We

Explore more at: www.liggywebb.com